AMONG

Angels

AMONG

Angels

POEMS BY

Nancy Willard & Jane Yolen

Illustrated by S. Saelig Gallagher

HARCOURT BRACE & COMPANY

New York   San Diego   London

For Frederick and Claske Franck—N. W.

To David Stemple, Angel of Archives—J. Y.

For Michael—S. S. G.

Grateful acknowledgement is made to the following for previously published material:
"An Angel Considers the Naming of Meat" and "The Mission of the Puffball" originally appeared in *Field*. "An Angel Tells the Birds to Gather for the Great Supper of God" and "A Carol for the Shepherds" originally appeared in *The Formalist*. "An Inconvenience of Wings" originally appeared in *Passages North*. "Angels among the Servants" and "The Winged Ones" originally appeared in *The New Yorker*. "Angels in Winter" from *Household Tales of Moon and Water*, copyright © 1987 by Nancy Willard, reprinted by permission of Harcourt Brace & Company. "Visitation in a Pewter Dish II" originally appeared in *Caliban*. "Gabriel Returns from the Annunciation" and "Tobias and the Fish" originally appeared in *Confrontation: The Literary Journal of Long Island University*. "Harpo and the Angel" originally appeared in *The Laurel Review*. "Angel in a Window" originally appeared in *The Gettysburg Review,* volume 8, number 1, and is reprinted here by permission of the editors. "The Lesson on Guardian Angels at Star of the Sea Elementary" originally appeared in *New Letters*. "Lucifer" and "Angels Fly" originally appeared in *Isaac Asimov's Science Fiction Magazine*. "Harahel Writes on the Head of a Pin" originally appeared in the *Catholic Library Association Journal*.

Library of Congress Cataloging-in-Publication Data
Willard, Nancy.
Among angels / by Nancy Willard and Jane Yolen.—1st ed.
    p.   cm.
ISBN 0-15-100195-2
1. Angels—Poetry. 2. American poetry—Women authors. 3. American poetry—20th century. I. Yolen, Jane. II. Title.
PS3573.I444A8   1995
811'.54—dc20   93-42103

PRINTED IN SINGAPORE
Designed by Michael Farmer
The text was set in Bembo.
First edition
A B C D E

Contents

AMONG

Angels

Prayer

Angel of lost spectacles
and hens' teeth,

angel of snow's breath
and the insomnia

of cats, angel
of snapshots fading

to infinity,
don't drop me—

shoeless,
wingless.

Defender of burrows,
carry me—

carry me
in your pocket of light.

—NANCY WILLARD

Pistis Sophia: A Dispatch

She took the twisting serpent in hand,
its tail twined around her arm;
pumping mighty wings she flew
along the trails of sky.
The garden was still except for the two
down by the river, naming the reeds.
She dropped the serpent by the apple tree,
then, following celestial orders,
flew back across the infinite blue.
Reports of strife on the back streets
and strikes by cherubim
occupied her long past the Fall.
In the Spring—she heard—
the two were served a sharp, swift eviction.
By then all Heaven was in an uproar,
so what did the Earth matter?

—JANE YOLEN

The garden was still except for the two/down by the river, naming the reeds.
—*Jane Yolen*

Angel among the Herbs

Angelica archangelica,
herb of the archangel Michael
on whose feast day you bloom,
you are not beautiful.

It is said that a monk
fell asleep and saw you,
tall, gawky,
singular as celery,

peering over the rose's shoulder,
the lily's cradle,
and woke singing
your praises.

You strengthen the heart,
unbind the lungs,
untrouble the stomach,
blow out bad spirits.

Let the juice of angelica
fall on deaf ears.
They will hear
the heartbeats of angels

and the dead coming back
in your roots
calling our names
in your green tongue.

—NANCY WILLARD

An Angel Considers the Naming of Meat

Whatever this was, with its arms and skirt,
crowned and winged and all-seeing,
it was no mere grazer. *Crown roast,*
butterfly chop, arm pot roast, skirt steak,
eye round. And what's left
is large and curious as a fallen tree,
split open, a breached tomb of roseate marble.
Seven ribs stand up in a sea of fat.
Like rowers they lean into the wind.
Once they rocked as one, in out, in out,
pushed by the breath of the living beast.
Now there is stillness
on the butcher's board, faintly hollowed
by the flesh of animals fallen under the knife

year after year. How can he bear it?
On his fluted rack hang hooks, poles,
a scraper for scrubbing the rough nap
off flesh ripped by the blade,
and a cleaver nipped from a halo of steel.
The electric slicer buzzes and whines,
but the plucked pullets sleep, curled up
in their chilly incubator,
their wings hugging their sides,
dreamless, having lost their heads.
If they had thumbs, they would be sucking them.
Famished, foolish, I am overcome with grief.
The butcher unhooks a sausage, cuts it,
hands me a wafer studded with precious meats.
"You're my first customer. This one's on me."

—NANCY WILLARD

Every visible thing in this world is put under the
charge of an angel.
—*St. Augustine*

Every Visible Thing

Asparagus I can believe,
in its first green thrust;
McIntosh apples, tart on the bough;
cardinals like a blot on winter's clean page;
raging crows on cropped fields.
Inching caterpillars I can believe,
fuzzy footed on a leafy spine;
trout rising at dusk,
shedding watered light;
willows weighted over with ice;
even the black snake winding
through the startled grass.
But what angel, totting eternities of
     poison ivy,
     snail darters,
     brussels sprouts,
could have time or will for exaltations?

—JANE YOLEN

Angels in Winter

Mercy is whiter than laundry,
great baskets of it, piled like snowmen.
In the cellar I fold and sort and watch
through a squint in the dirty window
the plain bright snow.

Unlike the earth, snow is neuter.
Unlike the moon, it stays.
It falls, not from grace, but a silence
which nourishes crystals.
My son catches them on his tongue.

Whatever I try to hold perishes.
My son and I lie down in white pastures
of snow and flap like the last survivors
of a species that couldn't adapt to the air.
Jumping free, we look back at

angels, blurred fossils of majesty and justice
from the time when a ladder of angels
joined the house of the snow
to the houses of those whom it covered
with a dangerous blanket or a healing sleep.

As I lift my body from the angel's,
I remember the mad preacher of Indiana
who chose for the site of his kingdom
the footprint of an angel and named the place
New Harmony. Nothing of it survives.

The angels do not look back
to see how their passing changes the earth,
the way I do, watching the snow,
and the waffles our boots print on its unleavened face,
and the nervous alphabet of the pheasant's feet,

and the five-petaled footprint of the cat,
and the shape of snowshoes, white and expensive as tennis,
and the deep ribbons tied and untied by sleds.
I remember the millions who left the earth;
it holds no trace of them

as it holds of us, tracking through snow,
so tame and defenseless
even the air could kill us.

—NANCY WILLARD

9

Angel in Summer: West Virginia

Forgiveness is water over stone,
twenty-one rocks till it is pure.
In my husband's home county
a river falls past strip mines,
over humpbacked boulders,
then is clear enough for trout.

I have eaten those rainbows,
small bones removed,
silver scales browned in butter,
startled eyes popped out.
Each time I ask forgiveness.

We are not afraid of the mountains,
riddled with rattlers.
An angel guides us through the passes,
along the switchbacks.
He looks like my dead father-in-law,
like a Viennese undertaker,
round-faced, small mustache.
He leaves no tracks.
While we fish the pools
he sits, melancholic on the shore;
there is no joy of heaven on his face,
his death too recent for absolution.
He smiles once, sadly, at a strike.

Each cast is a prayer.

—JANE YOLEN

The Mission of the Puffball

Unlike my brain, it was smooth
and white as that dead foam
they pack around porcelain
shipped from far ports.

Fat angel,
pocked like a wiffleball;
a racquet could send it spinning
into the trees,

but I did not harm it
because I never met
a guest so content
as that sly loaf rising

under the dark leaves
of the hosta,
ripening like cheese,
drawing from darkness

the alien moon of its flesh.
Ferns packing up for the winter
willingly left their shadows
with an angel sent to bare

God's inscrutable light:
  in the name of the snow
  and my white bowl of darkness,
  do as the air tells you.

—NANCY WILLARD

Names

The cherubs at the manger
have no names.
Anonymous,
they hang from the rafters,
singing out only
God's own.
I will call this one
Hosannah,
and that one
Hark,
and the little one
by the window,
wings ruffling
in the winter wind,
I shall call
Collie,
for, like a dog
rounding up sheep,
it was he chevied
poor shepherds on the hill,
driving them down
through narrowing streets
into the waiting fold.

—JANE YOLEN

A Carol for the Shepherds

An angel woke three shepherds
with timbrel, harp, and drum.
"The morning stars are singing,
the planets dance and hum.
So take yourselves to Bethlehem.
The Prince of Peace has come."

The sheep scattered behind them.
The crags were dark and wide.
"The wolves will surely find them.
We will not leave their side
for all the babes in Bethlehem,"
the frightened shepherds cried.

The angel sang, "O Morning Bright"
and from his sleeve let fall
a hundred stars, and by their light
the frightened shepherds saw
the wolf that watched their flocks by night
was caring for them all.

"Tonight the rivers sing for joy,
the very stones have tongues,
the lion and the lamb lie down,
the moon marries the sun.
So take yourselves to Bethlehem.
The Prince of Peace has come."

—NANCY WILLARD

An Angel Tells the Birds to Gather for the Great Supper of God

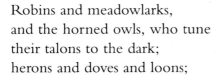

Robins and meadowlarks,
and the horned owls, who tune
their talons to the dark;
herons and doves and loons;

birds molting like the moon,
who turns her speckled face
on fields of empty space;
blackbirds whose polished wings

God nicked with holy fire;
and birds with names not heard
on any singer's mouth—
fly to the feast,

from north and south,
from west and east.

—NANCY WILLARD

Dancing with Angels

I am flat-footed, left-footed,
my heel narrower than my toes.
Slippery surfaces defeat me.
When I was younger
my *port de bras* carried me
through the lower grades.
Mr. B. smiled on me,
so like a god.
I danced with angels,
their wild wings in fourth position,
our toe shoes *slip-slip-slapping*
on the heads of pins.

—JANE YOLEN

Aunt Fanny

They were introduced, Mother said,
by a holy angel,
so what she was wearing a *shmata*
on her gray hair,
three black hairs protruding
from her chin.
She sucked lemons at night,
the room smelling like air freshener,
and she snored, a regular little engine.
Her shoes were always broken-down—
bunions, Mother said.
She made applesauce the old way,
from sour apples, could curl your tongue up.
At weddings she danced by herself,
all in a circle, clockwise;
at funerals she wept holding
the hands of other mourners.
She made a *shidekh,* it stuck, though,
so all the rest was forgiven.
Matchmakers are allowed
their little peculiarities,
like angels their wings, their halos.

—JANE YOLEN

Harpo and the Angel

The manager gave me a harp
who cried on my shoulder,
the left one, as I hunted and picked,
pondered and plucked.

She wanted to be a tree again,
to sing in a thousand tongues,
leaves tilting in the wind.
Now in the dark theater

she went speechless with grief
and showed me the syntax of silence,
its flowers and perfumes,
its chasms of light.

I was her silent brother,
even on Broadway. After one year
I could play "Annie Laurie."
When the crowd cried *encore*

I played it again.
Halfway home, I lost myself
in the crammed windows
of F. W. Woolworth and his

framed pictures, so cheap
even I could afford
the Grand Canyon,
a clipper at full sail,

my own face in the glass,
everything washed in heavenly light,
and nothing with a right to it, except
an angel in the middle,

as comfortable on her cloud
as if she were waiting for the bus
and to make the time go faster
playing her harp, which she leaned

against her right shoulder,
showing me how to hold my harp,
knowing what I needed to know,
and giving me private lessons.

—NANCY WILLARD

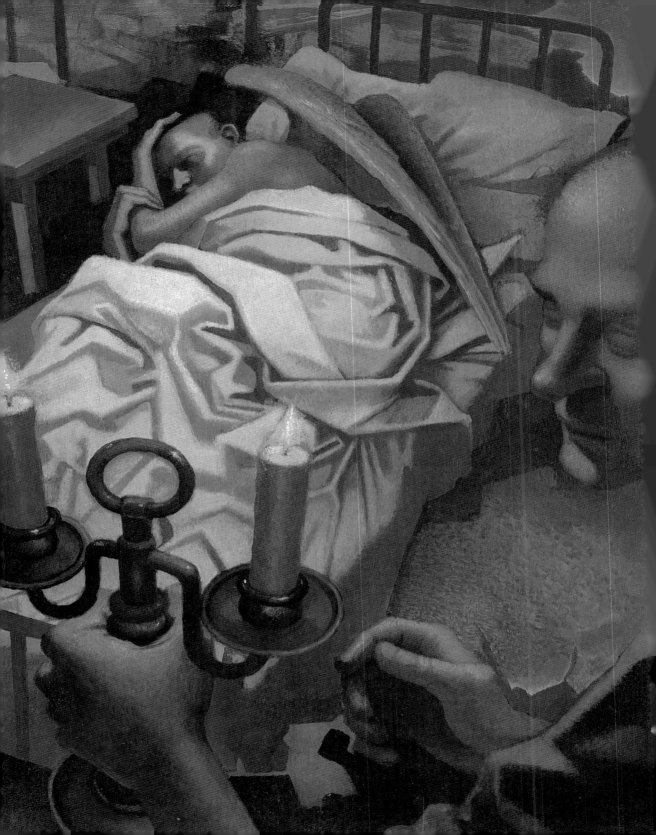

An Inconvenience of Wings

In my book of prayers I studied
the picture of Saint Peter, leather apron,
keys at his belt, waking the souls
in their heavenly orphanage.

On the nightstand by each bed
gleams a blue pitcher,
a white cup, and candlestick.
It is clean there.

Six souls share the ewer and basin,
soap and towel. Between their cots
twelve slippers nap side by side
like cats on the cloud floor.

It is cold there. The souls curl
under their quilts, wings hugging
their backs. How terrible for them
when a foot tingles,

a wing turns pins and needles.
"Growing pains," my mother said
when leg cramps staggered me from bed.
"Stand up. Put your weight on it."

—NANCY WILLARD

Angels fly because they take themselves lightly.
—*G. K. Chesterton*

Angels Fly

Angels fly
because
they take themselves
lightly between the thumb
and forefinger,
and lift themselves
above the casual world.

Angels fly
because
they take themselves
lightly as flour on a board,
rising in yeasty splendor
into the bowl of the sky.

Angels fly
because
they take themselves
lightly as sun
on dark water,
breaking into motes
that float along the tumbling stream.

Angels fly
because
they take themselves
lightly above
the gravity
of any situation.

Angels fly
because
they take themselves
lightly.

—JANE YOLEN

The Winged Ones

No birthday gift whiter or stranger
than this large pair of wings
my son bought on Amsterdam Avenue.
Pressed from celluloid, thick
as a toenail; two basins
that crease the morning light
in deeply stamped feathers.
A fossil from heaven. The tag
warns: "Not intended for flight."

"One size fits all," you assure me
and unfold the intricate harness
and buckle the wings to my body
that never sprang from a sill
or plotted the air through a thicket
or turned on the lathe of a wind
that could snuff out the breath in me
and toss me out of my garden.
There's no finer sight in summer

than yourself wearing them,
making the rounds in Eden,
inspecting the spotted throat
of the lily, the fern's plumage,
stepping behind your girl
quiet as mint on the move
in the woods where the owl lives
and hugging her where the gate was,
angel who forgives.

—NANCY WILLARD

Metamorph

I have given away my wings;
a feather on the mantle reminds me;
each bird song recalls that transformation.
My shoulders, like a mother's memory book,
hold aches as painful as old photographs.
Nothing, nothing is truly given away.
When Lucifer streaked across
God's clean sky,
we did not see the writing on it
for a thousand thousand
light-stained years.

—JANE YOLEN

Angel Feather

Here is the quill,
Here the vane,
A hymnal of ivory,
A canticle of bone.
We rise with the light,
Benedicte to the dawn,
Dive arrow-slim into the East
And with a prayer—

                         gone.

—JANE YOLEN

Angel in a Window

Night has fallen in Gethsemane so fast
it bruises the lilies of the field.
Over the altar, the angel

in tailored moss and russet wings
still hovers above the acolyte
who touches his wand to the tapers

and wakes them for vespers.
With their brass collars turned,
two flames bow to each other.

In the dark suburbs
to the right of the altar
prayer candles flicker among themselves

like deaf children in the park
after supper, waiting
for the big lights to wake
over the empty field.

—NANCY WILLARD

Lucifer

Turning and turning,
He falls fair
Into the morning,
Below God's laughter;
Feathers like fingers
Clutching the air,
Dragging and dragging
Fell night after.

—JANE YOLEN

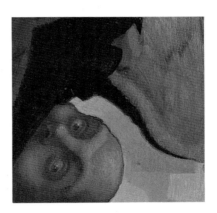

oh, the depth of the riches of
the wisdom and knowledge
of god.
Romans - 11:33

Easter Sermon

Do not mention angels, I am warned.
Unitarians do not believe.
My talk, therefore, is of a feral child,
mute in its wild agonies,
given no tongue by God
but the raven's,
the nightjar's,
the spotted snake's,
the wolf's.
Overhead a fan, like angel wings,
beats out a different tale.
The children gaze upward;
the adults stare down at their feet.
Afterward, each confession whispers into my ear:
"I believe in angels."
"I believe."

Someone flies heavenward from church,
laughter floating down like feathers,
like sermons from the sky,
I believe.

—JANE YOLEN

Harahel Writes on the Head of a Pin

Hunched by the candle,
wings humped behind,
the angel of archives
scribbles his prayers.
Shema Yisroel
one hundred thousand times;
the tiny consonants
lumining his face,
his chin so bearded
with the light,
passing cherubim
mistake him for
God.

It is always thus
with writers.

—JANE YOLEN

Gabriel Returns from the Annunciation

Notice the wings of the angel
streaming from his body as he crosses

the open palms of the water.
When the ocean shows him

her many little knives,
his wings tremble and fray,

and the salt diamonds them.
They open like valves of light.

—NANCY WILLARD

Angelic Script

In the year 1327,
no longer happy with buttressed Gothic,
angels developed their own script.
Teiazel, tired of men of letters,
created two fonts:
Celeste and Malachim:
from *aleph* to *taw*
the serifs soared like comet heads
on the stands of each stroke.
You do not believe me?
It is so written
in the *Dictionary of Angels,*
and such volumes do not repeat lies.

—JANE YOLEN

The Founding of Saint Andrews

Brother Regulus awoke,
the light in his cell like dawn.
An angel squatted in it,
robe hitched up to his heavenly knees.
"Regulus," the angel said
in a voice so like fire,
one of his glorious eyebrows
was slightly singed with smoke.
"Bring the tooth. Kneecap, too.
Don't forget the upper armbone,
three fingers from the right hand."
Even for saintly relics,
it was a peculiar shopping list.
Pro forma, Regulus protested.

Then he got the bones.

They won for the Church this headland,
so like lost Eden,
where once boars rutted through gorse;
and lapwings, in huge straggling flocks,
darkened the winter air.
Now golfers play in packs across the green,
under clouds like riffling wings,
crying "Allelujah" with every putt.

God's angels know what they are about.

—JANE YOLEN

The Lesson on Guardian Angels
at Star of the Sea Elementary

Sister Humiliana, sparrow
shaken from His dark sleeve
to watch over children

like rows of new corn
till God shall call you,
to keep His letters in line

aleph, beth, gimel,
and camels, elephants,
and children,
each holding the apron strings
of the one in front of it—

Sister Liberata, hummingbird
that forgot how to walk,
in the photograph on the playground

you flap starched wings.
Your white habit is the laundry
of angels. Behind you,

Lake St. Clair unwinds
her wicked spools.
A storm is rising.

By this time you have both
crossed the equator into heaven,
leaving flocks of children
like shells at high tide
waiting for the whitecaps
to collect them.

—NANCY WILLARD

The Twenty-eight Angels Ruling in the Twenty-eight Mansions of the Moon

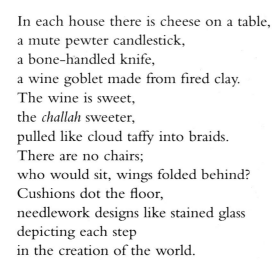

In each house there is cheese on a table,
a mute pewter candlestick,
a bone-handled knife,
a wine goblet made from fired clay.
The wine is sweet,
the *challah* sweeter,
pulled like cloud taffy into braids.
There are no chairs;
who would sit, wings folded behind?
Cushions dot the floor,
needlework designs like stained glass
depicting each step
in the creation of the world.

Come, eat, you are too thin.
God likes his angels like apples,
plump in their autumn skins.

—JANE YOLEN

Build a chair as if an angel
were going to sit on it.
—*Thomas Merton*

Angels among the Servants

St. Zita, patron saint
of scrub buckets and brooms,
spiritual adviser to mops,
protector of charwomen,
chambermaids, cooks,
those who wait on us
and mend our ways,

for forty-eight years you
lit the morning fire
in the dark kitchen
of Fatinelli of Lucca
and baked his bread,
till the Sunday you knew
you could not serve

two masters and did not open
the bins of flour or unlock
the treasures of yeast
and water. Telling no one,
you trudged off to Mass,
still wearing his keys
on your belt.

And while you opened your mouth
for the wafer, a coin
minted from moonlight,
angels arrived in aprons
and mixed light and salt,
and kneaded loaf after loaf,
punching them down

for their own good,
and praised the mystery
of bread, which rises to meet
its maker. But who
is the servant here?
The loaf will not rise
till the baker follows
the rules set down by the first loaf

for the ancient order of bread.
St. Zita, bless the fire
that boils water, the air
that dries clothes, and keys
that have lost their doors:
may angels keep them
from the deep river.

—NANCY WILLARD

Photographing Angels

for Lilo Raymond

The first angel you brought us stands high
over a city which does not appear in the picture,
yet no one who sees the angel doubts
the city is there. He folds his arms,
swathed in stone, and turns his blank gaze to heaven.
His hair seems newly hatched, snaky curls,
his wings chunky as bread, the feathers cast
from a mold like a big cookie.
When he clarified himself in your darkroom,
you saw what the lens did not show you:
a fly perched on an angel's head.

The second angel you brought us slumps
on a wall by a dump which does not appear in the picture.
Broken from the start, she will never be whole
except in the eye of the beholder
who praises the mosaic painter's art,
though bricks and cement cake
the hem of her robe like a scab. Her head on her hand,
her eyes closed, her wings ashen, she drags her dark torch
on the ground like a broken umbrella.
She has sunk so far into herself not even you
could bring her to brightness,

———————

though you brought her out of hiding.
Those years you photographed white curtains blowing
in white rooms over beds rumpled like ice floes,
you were honing your eye for what might dwell
in space as pure and simple as an egg.
The third angel you gave us holds a rose
so lightly it must have grown in a bed
where each rose chooses the hand that plucks it
and turns its open gaze on what rises and sets,
like a camera gathering the souls of pears,
the piety of eggs, the light in a dark room. Angels.

—NANCY WILLARD

Jacob Boehme and the Angel

I
A light in his workshop
unlocked his sleep and, fearing
a fire, the shoemaker
ran barefoot

across the snow
and opened the door.
The angel was waiting
on sapphire feet.

The shoemaker measured,
marked, and cut. Soles,
foxing, and tips fell
from the burnished calfskin,

laid to rest on the wooden last,
like a foot unfit for walking.
He crimped and stitched,
and the angel watched,

and the shop grew hot
as a foundry. He threaded
his needle with fire,
and with fire nailed heel

to sole, and with fire
pulled the shoes
from the last. The angel
put them on,

first the left,
then the right,
stepping so softly
even the snow did not speak of it.

—NANCY WILLARD

Visitation in a Pewter Dish

II

When Jacob finished stitching
the seventh pair of shoes,
his hands smelled of new
leather, as if the calf
whose mortal part he'd shaped
wanted to claim him.

Five blind bells woke
the fields at the edge of town.
Men left off binding the rain
into shocks of gold and rested
at noon under the plane trees.
    Angelus Domini—
The cows were happy boulders,

and Jacob saw, in a pewter dish
on a dirty table, seven angels
lapped in their own light.
Prove all things, sang the dish.
Hold fast to that which is good.
Jacob said nothing, only watched

with great joy. Wheels clattered
on the cobbled streets.
Two customers paid with gold,
two with wool, three with pork,
and the shoes took their first steps
out of the fields of light.

—NANCY WILLARD

Jacob and the Angel

The chandelier of stars
hung low above the field
when the angel closed on him.
He could not pry
porphyritic fingers
from his thigh,
nor break the granite hold.
Stone has no heart for pity.
He was lamed before night's end,
named before dawn;
shriven, driven, broken, repaired.
The angel could have gone on and on.
God asks much for little,
little for much.
We who have no choice must choose:
to win, to lose,
to wrestle with angels.

—JANE YOLEN

49

For the Angel of Death is forbidden to take a man while he is engaged in
the study of Torah.
—from "Rabbi Loew and the Angel of Death" in Howard Schwartz's
Lilith's Cave

Rabbi Loew and the Angel of Death

Leaving his studies,
sweet as honey,
thick as bread,
Reb Loew spies a figure
at the temple,
a long shadow
amid long shadows,
sharp knife readying
above the scroll of names.

Do not tremble,
Reb Loew,
your hand will save the multitudes,
your will
will halt the plague.

Leaving his studies,
sweet as new cream,
thick as wine,
Reb Loew spies a figure
in his study,
a small light
amid small lights,
single white rose
in his childish palm.

52

Do not tremble,
Reb Loew,
your hand will save your grandson,
your will
will vault the heavens,

and all the angels but one
will dance the letters of your name.

—JANE YOLEN

And when the young man went down to wash himself, a fish leapt
out of the river, and would have devoured him.
—*Tobit, VI: 2.*

Tobias and the Fish

Grab this fish by the gills, said the angel,
and draw him to you, as if he came

by appointment to watch
our dry light drench his interior

castle, unshuttered at last.
Slit open the envelope of his flesh.

Lay his heart on a bed of coals.
When bad dreams trouble you,

the smoke's thin fingers
will scroll up your sorrow.

Even the gall of this fish unclouds
eyes whited over with grief.

Alive, he swam beside us
and calmed the dark waters.

—NANCY WILLARD

The Archangel Michael Delivers a Sermon to the Stars

Mercury, Venus, the dancing sisters,
you think you spin in endless ellipses;
there is an end.
Saturn, Jupiter, the stars that touch
nose of bear, hunter's arrow,
ram's bright horns,
there is an end.
Uranus, Neptune, the bull's hooves,
the bright fish tail,
there is an end.
All you stars and constellations,
all you black holes and planetary nations,
there is an end.
The heavens are but a bright orrery
set in motion by the breath of God.

—JANE YOLEN